In the Footsteps of Explorers

Sir John Franklin

The Search for the Northwest Passage

Anders Knudsen

Crabtree Publishing Company

www.crabtreebooks.com

Crabtree Publishing Company

www.crabtreebooks.com

To my parents

Coordinating editor: Ellen Rodger
Series editor: Carrie Gleason
Project editor: L. Michelle Nielsen
Editor: Adrianna Morganelli
Design and production coordinator: Rosie Gowsell
Cover design, layout, and production assistance: Samara Parent
Art direction: Rob MacGregor
Scanning technician: Arlene Arch-Wilson
Photo research: Allison Napier
Prepress technician: Nancy Johnson

Consultant: Tracey L. Neikirk, Museum Educator, The Mariners' Museum

Photo Credits: Derrick Francis Furlong/Alamy: p. 31 (right); Wolfgang Kaehler/Alamy: p. 27; The Print Collector/Alamy: p. 23; Visual Arts Library (London)/Alamy: p. 16; World History Archive/Alamy: p. 11; Royal Geographical Society, London, UK/The Bridgeman Art Library: p. 14, p. 18; The Stapleton Collection, Private Collection/The Bridgeman

Art Library: pp. 6-7, p. 10, p. 13, p. 25; Corbis: p. 19, p. 20; Galen Rowell/Corbis: p. 30; The Granger Collection, New York: cover, p. 15; Mary Evans Picture Library / The Image Works: p. 9; Topham/The Image Works: p. 17 (top left); North Wind/North Wind Picture Archives: p. 5.

Illustrations: Dennis Gregory Teakle: p.4

Cartography: Jim Chernishenko: title page, p. 12

Cover: Every member of Franklin's final expedition to find the Northwest Passage died during the journey.

Title page: Franklin sailed across the Atlantic Ocean three times to find the Northwest Passage. During his first two journeys he treked over land, as well as as rivers, and the Actic Ocean. For his final trip, he traveled mostly through the harsh waters of the Arctic Ocean.

Sidebar icon: Snowshoes were used by Native Americans, including the Inuit, and European explorers to trek across the snowy terrain of northern North America.

Library and Archives Canada Cataloguing in Publication

Knudsen, Anders
    Sir John Franklin : the search for the Northwest Passage / Anders Knudsen.

(In the footsteps of explorers)
Includes index.
ISBN 978-0-7787-2420-9 (bound)
ISBN 978-0-7787-2456-8 (pbk.)

    1. Franklin, John, Sir, 1786-1847--Juvenile literature.
2. Explorers--Great Britain--Biography--Juvenile literature. 3. Northwest Passage--Discovery and exploration--British--Juvenile literature.
4. Canada, Northern--Discovery and exploration--British--Juvenile literature. I. Title. II. Series.

FC3961.1.F73K58 2007   j917.1904'1092   C2007-900663-9

Library of Congress Cataloging-in-Publication Data

Knudsen, Anders.
    Sir John Franklin : the search for the Northwest Passage / written by Anders Knudsen.
        p. cm. -- (In the footsteps of explorers)
    Includes index.
    ISBN-13: 978-0-7787-2420-9 (rlb)
    ISBN-10: 0-7787-2420-4 (rlb)
    ISBN-13: 978-0-7787-2456-8 (pb)
    ISBN-10: 0-7787-2456-5 (pb)
    1. Franklin, John, Sir, 1786-1847. 2. Explorers--Great Britain--Biography.
3. Arctic regions--Discovery and exploration--British. 4. Northwest Passage--Discovery and exploration--British. I. Title. II. Series.

G660.K68 2007
910.9163'27--dc22
                                                            2007003406
                                                                 LC

Crabtree Publishing Company

www.crabtreebooks.com   1-800-387-7650

Published in Canada
Crabtree Publishing
616 Welland Ave.
St. Catharines, ON
L2M 5V6

Published in the United States
Crabtree Publishing
PMB16A
350 Fifth Ave., Suite 3308
New York, NY 10118

Published in the United Kingdom
Crabtree Publishing
White Cross Mills
High Town, Lancaster
LA1 4XS

Published in Australia
Crabtree Publishing
386 Mt. Alexander Rd.
Ascot Vale (Melbourne)
VIC 3032

Contents

An Arctic Adventurer

Sir John Franklin was an Arctic explorer who sailed for Great Britain's Royal Navy. He was sent on expeditions to find the Northwest Passage, a sailing route through the present-day Canadian Arctic Ocean. During his third attempt to find the passage, he and his crew mysteriously vanished.

The Northwest Passage

Many explorers had tried to find the Northwest Passage before Franklin. They believed it would be a quicker route to Asia than the existing routes, one of which had them sailing around the southern tip of South America. In Asia, traders could get spices, silks, and other goods that could be sold for a lot of money in Europe. In Franklin's time, people no longer believed a Northwest Passage could provide a quicker route to Asia but explorers still hoped to map it because it was one of the last uncharted places in the world.

Franklin's Contribution

Franklin was interested in sea exploration from a young age, and took part in many voyages that traveled all over the world. In 1818, Franklin sailed on his first voyage to the Arctic Ocean. Over the next 26 years he went on three Arctic expeditions to find the Northwest Passage. He succeeded in mapping much of North America's northern coastline. In 1845, Franklin led a voyage to map the last remaining uncharted piece of coastline, but, after being spotted in mid-summer by **whalers**, Franklin, his crew, and two ships disappeared.

During Franklin's lifetime, he (above), and other explorers, were among the most famous people in the world.

The Rescue Effort

In total, over 40 rescue expeditions were sent to find Franklin and his men. These rescue missions succeeded in mapping a great deal of the Arctic region, but did not find Franklin. Franklin's second wife, Lady Jane Franklin, helped organize many rescue parties. She wrote letters to anyone she thought could help her, including the president of the United States. One of her letters to the president, written in the style of the day, was published in the *New York Times* newspaper.

"... I know that my surest ground of hope is in the prompting of a great people's humanity towards the suffering and forlorn navigators ... I seek only the rescue of a beloved husband and of his brave and devoted companions and followers, many of whom are my friends - all of whom are my countrymen. When I saw them depart, full of self devotion and enthusiasm, I promised myself, if need should ever be, to strive to save them,... Helpless myself, to redeem the pledge, I seek to move the hearts of others."

~ Lady Jane Franklin

Many ships, including the one below, coming from a number of countries were involved in the search for John Franklin.

- April 16, 1786 -

John Franklin is born in Spilsby, England.

- 1819 -

Franklin sets sail on his first of three voyages to find the Northwest Passage.

- June 11, 1847 -

Franklin dies in the Arctic.

- 1847 to 1859 -

Over 40 rescue missions are sent to find Franklin and his crew.

In Search of a Passage

From the early 1500s, European explorers had dreamed of discovering a Northwest Passage that would lead to the Pacific Ocean, and act as a short cut to Asia. The British were especially eager to find it and sent expeditions by land and sea.

By Sea

The first explorers who tried to find the Northwest Passage did so on ships, mapping many of the islands, bays and inlets of the Arctic. Henry Hudson was an English explorer who discovered Hudson Bay, an **inland sea** in present-day north central Canada, in 1610. Five years after Hudson's voyage, another English explorer, William Baffin, mapped much of the largest island in the Canadian Arctic, later named Baffin Island. While both Hudson and Baffin failed to find the passage, the maps they and others made were useful to later explorers who continued the search for the passage.

By Land

Other explorers traveled over land and river, looking for a route to the Pacific Ocean, which separated North America and Asia. Most of these men were hired by **trading companies**, such as the Hudson's Bay Company, or HBC. In 1769, Samuel Hearne, an English explorer, was sent to chart the rivers of northern North America. Hearne followed the Coppermine River, which is in present-day Northwest Territories, Canada, all the way to the Arctic Ocean, but he did not find a route to the Pacific.

(background) British explorer William Parry went on three voyages to find the Northwest Passage between 1819 and 1823. His crew often spent the winters in the Arctic, waiting for icy waters to melt.

A Renewed Quest

The expeditions of William Baffin and other explorers showed that even if the Northwest Passage existed, it would be a difficult route to navigate because of the harsh climate. Few voyages were sent by the British Navy after Baffin's voyage until they once again became interested in Arctic exploration more than 200 years later. By this time, the purpose of the search for the Northwest passage was not to find a quicker route to Asia but a challenge to discover uncharted lands.

Deep into the Arctic

In 1819, Captain William Parry, a Royal Navy officer, sailed deep into the North American Arctic Ocean. No one had ever sailed so far west into the Arctic. Parry discovered that there were many islands throughout the area, which would make finding a route to the Pacific Ocean difficult. His crew spent the winter in the Arctic, his ships trapped in ice. They hunted caribou and other animals for food, and also ate canned meats and vegetables. Parry hoped to reach the Pacific Ocean the following summer, but the waters to the west remained ice, and no passages could be found to the south. Parry was forced to sail home to England.

Lessons at Sea

John Franklin was born in Spilsby, England, in 1786. His father hoped he would become a church minister but John knew that he was bound for the sea. At 12 years old, he joined the crew of a merchant **ship**, and by the age of 14 he had joined the Royal Navy.

Family Connections

In 1801, Franklin received a post on the **HMS** *Investigator*, a ship captained by his uncle, Matthew Flinders, an explorer and cartographer, or mapmaker. Flinders hoped to circumnavigate, or sail around, Australia and make maps. Two years into the voyage, the ship began to rot, forcing the expedition to land and change ships. While sailing back to England in 1803, the ship Franklin was on was shipwrecked on a reef. Franklin and many of the crew were stranded on a sand bar for 51 days before being rescued. Franklin made it home on a merchant ship, arriving in London in 1804.

Rising through the Ranks

After returning to England, Franklin served for three years on the *Bellerophon*, a navy warship. During Franklin's time on board, the ship was involved in battles against France, including the Battle of Trafalgar, an important victory for Great Britain during the Napoleonic Wars, which had begun four years earlier. Franklin then joined the *Bedford*, another navy ship, in 1807, where he was made lieutenant. The *Bedford* sailed around the world, including to South America, the **West Indies**, and the **North Sea**. When Franklin returned to England, the Napoleonic Wars were ending and the Navy did not need as many officers. Franklin went home and spent the next few years with his family.

Franklin joined the Investigator *in 1801 as a midshipman. He was taught to draw maps, and use navigational instruments, such as a compass (above) and an octant (left).*

Napoleonic Wars

The Napoleonic Wars were a series of battles led by France between 1800 and 1815. Under the command of Napoleon Bonaparte, the emperor of France, the French armies succeeded in taking over many countries in Europe. Great Britain's greatest defense against attack was their Royal Navy, which prevented Napoleon's armies from reaching Great Britain. British troops defeated Napoleon in 1815.

(background) During the Napoleonic Wars, few voyages of exploration were sent out by Great Britain because ships were needed in battle.

Eating Boots

When the Napolenic wars ended, the Admiralty Board, or the leaders of the Royal Navy, decided to once again fund voyages to the North American Arctic. In 1819, Franklin was sent to map an unexplored section of Arctic coastline.

Heading West

To reach the Arctic coastline, Franklin trekked across present-day Canada. On August 30, 1819, Franklin's crew arrived at York Factory, a HBC trading post on Hudson Bay. There, they picked up boats, food, and other supplies. Franklin hired **voyageurs** and Native Americans to act as guides and hunt for food. They spent most of the winter at a post in present-day northern Saskatchewan, Canada. The next spring, they traveled north, nearly 900 miles (1448 km), reaching Fort Providence, the most northerly trading post.

Mapping the Arctic

Continuing north, the expedition chose a spot south of the Coppermine River to build a new fort, called Fort Enterprise. It was not until early June 1821 that Franklin and his men headed north along the Coppermine River. Less than three weeks later they arrived at the river's mouth, where it meets the Arctic Ocean. Hoping to reach Hudson Bay, the group paddled east along the coastline.

In 1818, Franklin was a part of a crew sent to the North Pole. They did not make it past Spitsbergen (above), an island north of Norway.

Turning Back

In late August, after traveling 500 miles (805 kilometers) along the coastline and with food supplies running low, Franklin decided to head back to Fort Enterprise. Rather than paddling back through the rough Arctic waters, Franklin and his crew traveled over land through unexplored country. When their food supplies ran out, they were forced to eat wild berries, **lichen**, and animal skins, including their own leather shoes.

Rescued

Franklin had arranged to have a group of Native Americans restock Fort Enterprise with food, but when they arrived there was none. The men were too weak to continue. A group of Native peoples arrived in November. They gave the men food, and guided them back to York Factory. When Franklin arrived in England in the Fall of 1822, the story of his journey was already known. He was known as "the man who ate his own boots."

(background) Franklin's crew was made up of Navy officers, voyageurs, and Chipewyan Native peoples. By the time they reached Fort Enterprise on the return journey, some men had died from starvation and exhaustion.

Back to the Arctic

In 1823, Franklin got approval from the Admiralty Board for another expedition to map the Northwest Passage. This expedition divided into two groups, and each mapped an uncharted section of coastline.

Lessons Learned

Franklin hoped to avoid the problems he had during his last trip to the Arctic. Franklin arranged to carry more supplies, and to use stronger boats that were light, and sturdy enough to withstand floating ice and rough weather. Before Franklin's expedition began, a group of British officers was sent to the north of present-day Northwest Territories, Canada. They built a fort, which was named Fort Franklin, on the Mackenzie River, near Great Bear Lake, where Franklin's expedition spent the winter.

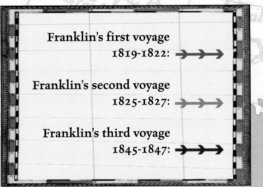

Franklin's first voyage
1819-1822:

Franklin's second voyage
1825-1827:

Franklin's third voyage
1845-1847:

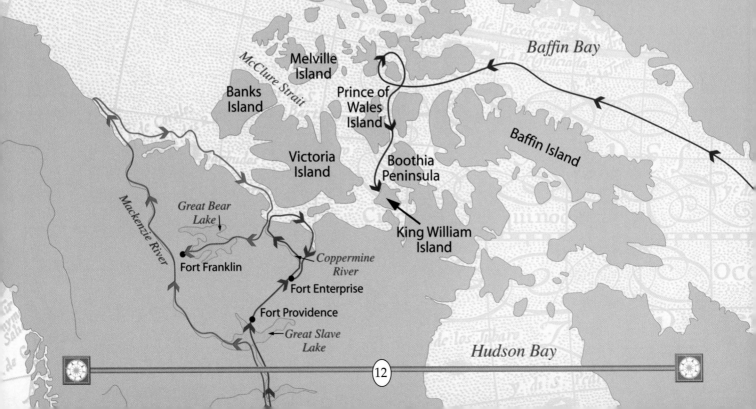

GREENLAND

Baffin Bay

Melville Island

McClure Strait

Banks Island

Prince of Wales Island

Baffin Island

Victoria Island

Boothia Peninsula

King William Island

Great Bear Lake

Mackenzie River

Fort Franklin

Coppermine River

Fort Enterprise

Fort Providence

Great Slave Lake

Hudson Bay

Overland to the Arctic

Franklin arrived at a naval post on Lake Huron in the spring of 1825. The expedition, with 33 men, traveled over land, rivers, and lakes. They stopped at forts along the way to pick up supplies, until they reached Fort Franklin. Over the winter, the officers studied the **geography** of the area. They also taught the voyageurs and sailors to read and write.

A Successful Return

The expedition left Fort Franklin in June, 1826, and headed north along the Mackenzie River, which took them to the Arctic Ocean. As they neared the Arctic Ocean, the expedition divided into two groups. Half the men traveled east along the Arctic coastline to the Coppermine River, 500 miles (805 kilometers) away. The rest went westward with Franklin. By late August, Franklin's group had traveled nearly 400 miles (644 kilometers), before they were forced by cold temperatures, rough winds and heavy fog to turn back and return to Fort Franklin. Even though Franklin did not make it as far west as he had hoped, the expedition was a great success. In his two expeditions to the North American Arctic, Franklin and his men mapped 1,878 miles (3,022 kilometers) of previously unexplored coastline.

The Inuit are Native peoples who live in the northern regions of present-day Canada, Alaska, and Greenland. Franklin met groups of Inuit peoples on both his first and second expeditions to find the Northwest Passage. Franklin's meetings with the Inuit were usually friendly. He brought trade items, such as beads and metal knives, to give to the Inuit. In return, the Inuit gave the expedition dried fish and meat.

A Final Attempt

When Franklin returned to England in 1827, he immediately wanted to organize another voyage to map the last unexplored section of Arctic coastline. The Admiralty Board rejected this idea. Instead, Franklin served in a number of government positions, including lieutenant governor of Van Diemen's Land, or the present-day island of Tasmania, Australia.

For his service, Franklin became a decorated officer. He received many awards and honors, including being knighted by Great Britain's king.

Renewed Hope

Franklin spent six years in Van Diemen's Land, returning to Great Britain in 1844. Soon after his return, he was chosen to lead another expedition to find the Northwest Passage. The Admiralty Board decided to send an expedition to map the last unexplored section of the Arctic, which lay to the west of Boothia Peninsula, a stretch of mainland that reaches into the Arctic Ocean.

Too Old?

Some of the Lords thought Franklin, at 58 years old, was too old to lead another expedition. Many Arctic explorers supported Franklin as the best man for the job because of his knowledge of the conditions and geography of the Arctic. The Admiralty Board chose Navy captain, Francis Crozier, to lead one ship, the *HMS Terror*, while Franklin was made captain of the *HMS Erebus*.

Prepared for the Arctic

Over 130 men volunteered to join Franklin's expedition. Arctic voyages were dangerous, and the Admiralty wanted only the most skilled sailors. They offered twice the regular sailor's wage. The ships were stocked with enough food to last three years, in case they got trapped in the ice and were forced to spend more than one winter in the Arctic. The supplies included a large number of preserved foods, such as canned vegetables and soup, salted meat, and pickles, which did not spoil on long voyages. There were also hunting rifles and fishing nets, so that the men could catch their own food if their supplies ran out.

Last Sight of the Expedition

The expedition left England on May 19, 1845. They sailed across the Atlantic Ocean and along the west coast of Greenland. In early July, the ships sent a package of letters home with a small freight ship that was heading back to Britain. The *Erebus* and *Terror* were seen again in late July by two whaling ships in Baffin Bay, a waterway between Greenland and the Arctic Archipelago. This was the last time Franklin and his men were seen by Europeans.

(background) Both the Erebus *and* Terror *had been war vessels. Iron plates were nailed to their bows to withstand the force of ice floes.*

The Search

After two summers passed without news from the expedition, rescue voyages were organized to look for Franklin and his men. Over the next twelve years, more than 40 expeditions, including search parties from Britain and the United States, went looking for Franklin.

Rescue Efforts

The first search parties were **funded** by the Royal Navy. The Navy had rescue ships enter the Arctic from the east and west. An expedition leaving in 1848 followed Franklin's route into the Arctic, spending the winter there. **Sledge** parties were sent over the ice to Arctic islands to look for Franklin but they found no sign of the expedition. Lady Jane Franklin, Franklin's second wife, also organized expeditions, and wrote to the Admiralty Board, Arctic explorers, and private businessmen, encouraging further efforts to find her husband.

Finding Bodies

Finally, in 1850, a group of rescue ships gathered near Beechey Island, a small island northwest of Baffin Island. Searchers discovered the graves of three members of Franklin's crew on the island. The inscriptions on the gravestones said the men died in early 1846. It is believed that these men died of **tuberculosis** and **scurvy**. Scurvy was a common disease for sailors and explorers to get. It is caused by a lack of vitamin C, which is found in fresh fruit and vegetables, foods that were not plentiful on long sailing journeys.

> (background) Many explorers survived in the Arctic by conserving food and hunting animals. This picture shows the crew of the Terror playing a game during an Arctic winter.

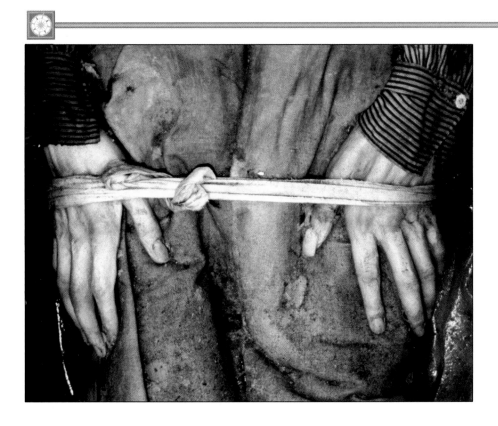

The Northwest Passage Discovered

In 1850, a number of search expeditions entered the Arctic from the Pacific Ocean. Robert McClure, a Royal Navy captain, discovered a passage between two westerly islands, Banks Island and Victoria Island, which he named Prince of Wales Strait. By sailing through this strait, he reached a frozen passage, which was later named McClure Strait. McClure and his men crossed this strait by sledge to reach Melville Island. This was the farthest spot previous explorers had reached from the east. By reaching Melville Island from the west, McClure discovered an important link in finding a northwest passage, allowing geographers to map the first complete passage. Franklin's plan had been to find a more southerly route, which would be easier to sail because it would not be frozen for as much of the year.

(above) In the early 1980s, scientists dug up three of Franklin's crew. The bodies were well preserved because of the cold climate. They found evidence the men died of lead poisoning. Lead in the solder that sealed food cans may have leaked into the food.

- May 19, 1845 -

Franklin and his crew sail from Britain on Franklin's third expedition to find the Northwest Passage.

- July 25, 1845 -
Franklin and his crew are last seen by sailors aboard whaling ships.

- 1854-
The Royal Navy sends its last search party to find Franklin.

- 1858 -
A search party, funded partly by Jane Franklin, discovers Franklin's fate.

Evidence of Tragedy

In 1854, explorer Dr. John Rae brought news of the fate of Franklin's expedition back to Great Britain. It was discovered Franklin's men had crossed the last unexplored section in the Arctic, making them, and not McClure, the first to find a northwest route through the Arctic.

John Rae

Dr. John Rae was sent by the Hudson's Bay Company to chart the west coast of Boothia Peninsula. Dr. Rae brought two interpreters who could speak English and Inuktitut, the language of the Inuit peoples. One group of Inuit told Rae's interpreters they met 40 British sailors on King William Island, an island west of Boothia Peninsula, in the spring of 1850. Later that spring, the Inuit said they found 30 dead bodies on the mainland of the continent.

Relics of Franklin's Expedition

The Inuit gave Dr. Rae a number of objects they had found near the bodies, including silver spoons that had the names of Franklin's officers engraved on them, proving they were telling the truth. When Rae returned to Great Britain with this information, he and his men were given a large reward by the British Government for discovering the fate of Franklin's expedition.

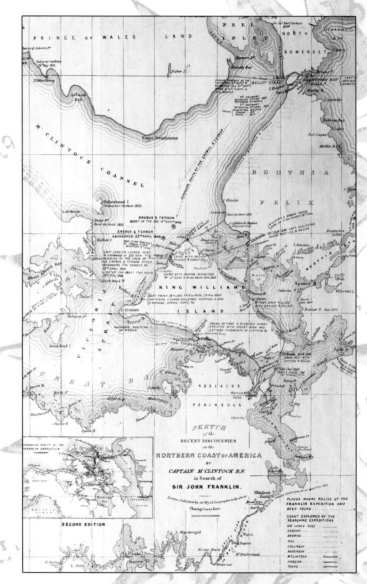

The expeditions in search of Franklin led to the mapping of not only the Northwest Passage but many of the islands in the Arctic Archipelago, or the islands north of the present-day Canada.

Jane Franklin Carries On

When news of Dr. Rae's discoveries reached Great Britain, Jane Franklin tried to organize another expedition to go to King William Island. Even if Franklin and his men were dead, Jane Franklin wanted to collect evidence proving that her husband and his men had discovered a northwest passage before they died. Jane Franklin convinced Francis Leopold McClintock, an experienced British Arctic explorer to captain the expedition. She bought a steam yacht, called the *Fox*, using her own money and donations from the public. She also convinced the Royal Navy to donate provisions and supplies. The expedition left England in the summer of 1857, and arrived at Boothia Pensinsula in September 1858.

McClintock's findings

McClintock's expedition sledged down the Boothia Peninsula. From the Inuit they came upon, McClintock's interpreter learned that a ship had been crushed by ice floes near King William Island, and another ship had been forced onto land. Along the north coast of King William Island, McClintock's men found cairns, or mounds of stones, built by some of Franklin's crew. Written reports sealed in metal cylinders were placed inside a cairn. One report, dated April 25th, 1848, had notes written in the margin and was signed by James Fitzjames, second-in-command of the *Erebus*. Fitzjames wrote, "Sir John Franklin died on the 11th of June 1847."

James Fitzjames' report said that the Terror and Erebus had been locked in ice off King William Island for two years, and that many of the men had died during their journey south to find help.

An Arctic Voyage

On Franklin's final voyage, his ships were outfitted with the most modern technology available. Steam engines were placed in the ships to help move them through ice channels. The ships carried a large supply of canned food, which at the time was a new method of preserving, or keeping, food.

The Terror and the Erebus

The *HMS Terror* and *HMS Erebus* were heavy, slow, and sturdy vessels. Their bows were lined with iron plates to protect them from being ruptured by ice. They relied mainly on sails, but each ship also had a steam engine that powered a propeller, helping to push the ship through the water. The **cabins** had hot water pipes fitted into the floors that heated the rooms. Each ship also carried a large stock of coal that was burned to heat the ship and run the steam engine.

A Gourmet Menu

Franklin brought enough supplies so that his crew would be comfortable for up to three years. The ships carried a lot of food, including canned meat, canned vegetables, 77 tons (70 tonnes) of flour, 3,700 gallons (14,000 liters) of liquor, and five tons (4.5 tonnes) of chocolate. The expedition was one of the earliest British voyages to have canned goods on board their ship. Unfortunately, the lead used in the cans may have caused lead poisoning in the crew, contributing to their deaths.

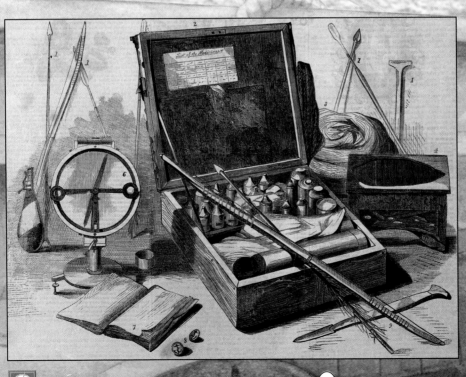

Many belongings of the Erebus and Terror crew were found by both Dr. John Rae and Captain Francis McClintock during their searches. These belongings included diaries, weapons, and compasses.

Canned Pickles

Pickling is a way to preserve foods. It is usually done by soaking cucumbers in a mixture of salt and an acidic liquid such as vinegar. Ask an adult to help you make pickles.

Ingredients:

4 pounds small, or pickling cucumbers

3 1/2 cups white vinegar

6 cups water

1/2 cup pickling salt

2 tablespoons sugar

8 cloves garlic, peeled

5 heads of fresh dill

2 tablespoons mustard seed

Directions:

1. Wash the cucumbers.
2. Mix the water, vinegar, salt, and sugar in a large pot, and heat until it boils.
3. Combine the dill, mustard seed, and garlic in a small bowl, and add an equal amount of the mixture to 4 one-quart (one-liter) mason, or canning, jars.
4. Put an equal number of cucumbers in each jar.
5. Add the boiling mixture to the jars, leaving 1/2 an inch (1 centimeter) of space at the top of the jar. Seal the jars tightly.
6. Carefully, place the jars in a pot of boiling water for 15 minutes.
7. Store them in a dark pantry until you have a pickle craving. After opening a jar of pickles, place it in the fridge.

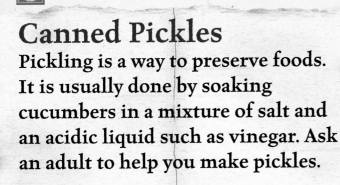

(background) Most of the men aboard the Erebus and Terror had never experienced the harsh conditions of the Arctic. Each man had a certain job to do, including sailors who did the physical work of sailing the ships, and surgeons who looked after the men's health.

It was believed that canning would keep foods such as vegetables fresh, preventing scurvy, a disease caused by a lack of vitamin C in the diet. Vitamin C is found in many vegetables.

Keeping Warm

Arctic explorers and sailors wore wool underwear and uniforms designed for cold weather. Most British sailors wore blue wool jackets over waistcoats, or vests. They also wore boots made of canvas lined with wool that had soles made of animal hide, or skin, and thick cotton or wool mittens. The cold temperatures of the Arctic often led to frostbite, or skin damage, which can cause the skin to tingle, blister, or turn gray. Frostbite often starts in the fingers and toes. John Rae, who discovered the fate of Franklin's expedition, used animal skins for clothing. He learned from the Inuit that caribou and seal skins were warmer than wool clothing.

(below) Some rescue parties searching for Franklin caught Arctic foxes and put collars around their necks that had messages attached to them. The messages stated the position of the search vessels. The searchers hoped Franklin's men would catch the foxes and discover the messages.

(background) The Arctic is made up mostly of the Arctic Ocean, which, in certain areas, is frozen all year. Icebergs are floating masses of ice. Many icebergs are pieces of glacier that break off when a glacier meets the ocean.

Wintering in the Arctic

When ships wintered in the Arctic, crew members built roofs over the decks that were made of wood, animal hide, or cloth, and covered in a layer of snow. This **insulated** the ship, protecting the men from the cold air and wind. Buildings were also constructed on the ice floes outside of the ship, including storerooms and **observatories**. These were built out of wood or snow and ice. To relieve boredom, the *Erebus* and *Terror* had musical instruments on board as well as libraries that were stocked with thousands of books on many subjects.

Sledges

Sledges were used by Arctic explorers when making treks over land or ice. Sledges are sled-like vehicles built to transport provisions and supplies. They are often made of wood, and use long metal or wood runners to glide across the snow or ice. In 1859, Francis McClintock discovered a sledge built by some crew members of the Franklin expedition who had been traveling down King William Island in search of help. It was made of a boat placed on wood runners. It weighed 1400 pounds (635 kilograms), and was filled with clothing, guns, and other supplies. The weakened men had been forced to abandon the heavy sledge.

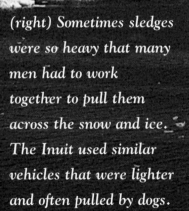

(right) Sometimes sledges were so heavy that many men had to work together to pull them across the snow and ice. The Inuit used similar vehicles that were lighter and often pulled by dogs.

The Inuit

Arctic explorers, including Franklin, met many different groups of Inuit people on their expeditions. When European explorers arrived, Inuit peoples lived in the Arctic from Alaska to Greenland, as well as many of the Arctic islands.

Inuit Ways of Life

The word "Inuit" means "the people," in the Inuit language of Inuktitut, of which there are many **dialects**. They have lived in the Arctic for thousands of years. Many Inuit were nomadic, or had no permanent homes. They moved from place to place, following **migrating** animals which were their main source of food.

Fishing and Hunting

The Inuit lived in bands, or groups of families. The leading hunter in the group would make many of the decisions, including what hunting grounds to travel to. The Inuit ate mainly meat, including fish, caribou, and whale. Seals were also a large part of their diet, which they hunted in the winter and spring. In the summer and fall they speared fish and hunted land animals. The Inuit ate most of their meat raw, but they also dried, boiled, and cooked their food.

To catch seals, a hunter waited by a breathing hole in the ice. When seals came up for a breath, the hunter struck them with a harpoon made of animal bone.

Waste Not, Want Not

The Inuit used every part of the animals they hunted. Bone was used to make tools, including ice chisels, spears and needles for sewing clothes. Animal skins were useful for making clothing and blankets. Sealskin, which is waterproof, was especially useful for boots, jackets, and the outside shells of **kayaks**. Caribou fur was especially warm. In winter, the Inuit wore two layers of furs, with the fur of the outside layer facing inward, to trap heat. Caribou sinew, or strong rope-like body tissue, was used to tie skins together.

Keeping Warm

In the winter, the Inuit lived in igloos. Igloos were dome-shaped, and made of blocks of snow and ice, with a low doorway or tunnel. Temperatures inside igloos were usually just below freezing, or 32° F (0° C), even when the temperature outside was much colder. Usually, more than one family lived in an igloo. The walls and floors were often lined with furs and skins. In the summer, hunting parties made tents using animal skins, supported by a frame made of bone and driftwood that they collected from the shoreline.

In winter, when Inuit hunters were away searching for food, they built igloos on ice floes to keep warm.

Huskies are the breed of dog that have pulled the sledges of the Inuit for thousands of years. Sled dogs spend all of their time outside and have a thick fur coat to keep them warm.

First Encounters

The first Europeans to encounter Inuit people were the Vikings, a people from northern Europe who explored and settled parts of Greenland around the year 1000. The English explorer Martin Frobisher, one of the first British explorers to travel to the Arctic, was the first European to describe a group of Inuit people, who he met in 1576 in the waters south of Greenland. On this voyage, Frobisher kidnapped an Inuit man and brought him back to England to show to the public. The man became ill and died.

Inuit Assistance

Franklin met Inuit people during his first expedition to the Arctic. He offered the Inuit gifts, including metal tools, to show he was friendly. The Inuit gave Franklin's men dried caribou meat, a welcome gift for the hungry men. Inuit groups also helped John Rae and Francis McClintock learn the fate of Franklin and his men. Both explorers were able to deal more successfully with the Arctic weather than Franklin's crew because they adopted Inuit ways of life, including wearing furs and animal skins to keep warm.

The Impacts of Trade

The Inuit had been trading with sailors aboard whaling ships since the early 1500s, when they exchanged food, furs, and whalebone for European-made goods, such as durable, or long-lasting, metal tools. As trade increased, European goods began to change Inuit ways of life. In places where whalers frequently visited, such as north of Hudson Bay, fishing nets and rifles slowly became more popular than Inuit spears and bows and arrows. Europeans also brought diseases to the Arctic, such as smallpox **and** influenza. The Inuit had never been exposed to these illnesses, so they had no immunity. It was difficult for them to fight off the diseases. Many Inuit died.

(background) While the Inuit adopted some European methods of hunting, including the use of rifles, they never gave up their traditional ways.

After Franklin

The rescue expeditions sent after Franklin succeeded in exploring and mapping large unexplored parts of the Arctic. Their efforts also proved that a Northwest Passage existed, but that the weather and ice conditions of the Arctic made this route very difficult to travel. In fact, no one successfully sailed the treacherous route until 1905.

Jane Franklin

After McClintock's return, Lady Jane Franklin did not fund any more rescue missions. In 1859, the Royal Geographical Society, an organization that promotes geographical discoveries, awarded her with a gold medal. The society praised her support of the rescue effort, and noted that her efforts had helped uncover the fate of her husband, as well as his discovery of the Northwest Passage.

Sailing the Northwest Passage

Franklin was a boyhood hero of Norwegian explorer, Roald Amundsen (1872 - 1928). In 1905, Amundsen became the first person to sail the entire Northwest Passage. Traveling in a fishing boat with a seven-person crew, Amundsen set sail at the age of 30. He followed the route Franklin took on his final voyage, avoiding the thick ice in the area where Franklin's ships were lost, and following the coastal route Franklin had helped map. Amundsen performed studies in the Arctic, including finding the location of the **North Magnetic Pole**. It took him almost three years to make the journey.

Six years after sailing the Northwest Passage, Amundsen became the first person to reach the South Pole, the most southerly point on Earth, on Antarctica.

A Culture Almost Destroyed

By 1900, the northern lands of North America, excluding Alaska, became territories of Canada. During the mid-1900s, the Canadian government encouraged the Inuit people to move to permanent settlements, rather than keeping their nomadic lifestyles. The government also believed they needed to be taught modern ways. Many children were taken from their families and forced to go to schools where they were taught in English, which they first had to learn. They were punished if they spoke Inuktitut or practiced native customs.

The Inuit today

The Inuit fought governments for rights to the northern lands they had lived on for thousands of years. In 1993, the Canadian government signed an agreement that transferred 217,500 square miles (350,000 square kilometers) of land to the Inuit. In 1999, this land became part of the territory of Nunavut. Nunavut covers a large part of the mainland as well as islands in the Arctic Archipelago. Schools in Nunavut teach in Inuktitut, as well as English, and provide programs that teach children about traditional Inuit ways of life.

Today, Inuit people from many different groups pride themselves in keeping their traditional ways of life alive. This woman is preserving fish by drying it in the sun.

An Arctic Legacy

Franklin's dedication to mapping the Northwest Passage, and his mysterious disappearance made him famous. When first discovered, the Northwest Passage was an almost unnavigable route. Today, it is used for about a month in the summer, when enough ice has melted, by a small number of ships. In the future it may become a busy shipping route.

The Northwest Passage Today

Today, the Northwest Passage is navigated by only a few ships, including Canadian Coast Guard icebreakers, research vessels, and ships carrying tourists. These ships are either ice-strengthened or icebreakers, designed to break through ice. Ice-strengthened ships can be any type of ship built to cope with icy waters but are not able to break through ice like icebreakers. They often have **double hulls** made of strong steel to prevent ice from puncturing their hulls.

Melting a Passage

Global warming is the gradual increase of temperatures on Earth. The increased temperatures cause ice in the Arctic to melt. Although scientists argue about when, they agree that sometime before 2090, the Northwest passage will be almost free of ice during the summer. An ice-free passage means **commercial** ships sailing between Europe and Asia will be able to sail a much shorter route than the current one that has them sailing to the Panama Canal in Central America.

(background) An icebreaker sailing through Arctic waters in the summer is still at risk of getting trapped by ice.

(left) Global warming is causing the ice floes, where polar bears live, to melt.

(below) This statue of John Franklin is located in Spilsby, England, where he was born.

Frankin Remembered

The story of Franklin's journeys were captured in poems and songs. Charles Dickens (1812 - 1870), a famous English writer, helped write a play based on Franklin's final expedition, called *The Frozen Deep*. Today, Franklin is honored in many countries. His name is linked to lakes, islands, rivers, mountains, and bays in Canada, including Franklin Strait, a waterway in the Arctic. In Hobart, the capital city of Tasmania, Australia, or the former Van Diemen's Land, a statue of Franklin stands in Franklin Square. Lady Jane Franklin succeeded in having a statue of her husband placed in Westminster Abbey, a famous church in London, England, where many kings and queens of Great Britain were crowned.

Glossary

cabins Inside rooms on board a ship

commercial Relating to businesses, which aim to make money

dialects A form of a language that is specific to an area or peoples

double hull A hull, or body of a ship, made of two layers of metal with a space in between the layers

forlorn Sad and lonely

funded Provided money for

geography The physical features of a land, including mountains and waterways

glacier A mass of ice that moves slowly across land

global warming An increase in temperatures on Earth partly caused by the sun's rays being trapped in the atmosphere by pollution

HMS Stands for His, or Her, Majesty's Ship; a title used for British Navy ships

ice floe A large sheet of floating ice

influenza A contagious disease with symptoms that include fever, aching muscles, and excess mucous in the throat, which affects breathing

inland sea A large body of salt water surrounded by land

insulated Trapped heat so an area or room would not drop in temperature

kayak A boat with a light wooden frame covered with watertight skins and propelled by a paddle

knighted To be made a knight, a title of high rank in British society

lead poisoning An illness caused by ingestion of the metal lead that can lead to death; symptoms include severe stomach pain and vomiting

lichen A fungus that grows on rocks or tree trunks

lieutenant governor The highest ranking government officer in a colony.

merchant Someone who buys and sells trade goods

migrating Moving from place to place

North Magnetic Pole The point on Earth compasses point to when they show the direction of north; the point moves and is south of the North Pole

North Sea The part of the Atlantic Ocean between Great Britain and the European continent

observatories Buildings that contain scientific equipment used to observe space, weather, and other scientific events

octant A tool used to determine a ship's position

redeem To fulfill or carry out

sledge A sled-like vehicle often pulled by dogs or other animals and used to transport cargo

small pox A disease that causes fever and pustules, or puss-filled blisters, to form on the skin

solder A metal that is melted and used to attach two or more metal pieces together

steam engine An engine powered by steam; in the past, the steam was often created by burning wood or coal

trading companies Companies that sold items found in North America, especially furs, in Europe

tuberculosis A contagious disease that causes fever, wasting of body tissue, and lung problems

voyageurs Men working for trading companies, who traveled to distant posts in North America to trade for furs and other goods with Native Americans

West Indies The Caribbean Islands, which lie between North and South America

whalers Sailors who hunt whales

Index

Printed in the U.S.A.